Fossil
Seekers

By Laura Buller

Series Literacy Consultant
Dr Ros Fisher

PEARSON
Longman

Pearson Education Limited
Edinburgh Gate
Harlow
Essex CM20 2JE
England

www.longman.co.uk

ISBN 0 582 84544 0

Colour reproduction by Colourscan, Singapore
Printed and bound in China by Leo Paper Products Ltd.

The Publisher's policy is to use paper manufactured from sustainable forests.

10 9 8 7 6 5 4 3

DK

The following people from **DK** have
contributed to the development of this product:

Art Director Rachael Foster

Nick Avery, Ann Cannings **Design**	**Managing Editor** Scarlett O'Hara
Cynthia Frazer, Helen McFarland **Picture Research**	**Editorial** Steve Setford, Kate Pearce
Richard Czapnik, Andy Smith **Cover Design**	**Production** Rosalind Holmes
David Lambert **Consultant**	**DTP** David McDonald

Dorling Kindersley would like to thank: Carole Oliver for additional design work and Jo Dixon for border artwork.

Picture Credits: American Museum Of Natural History: 14tl, 17t, 18b, 18t, 19t. Ardea London Ltd: © D.Parer & E.Parer Cook 5br. Art Directors &
TRIP: M. Lee 10–11b. Associated Press AP: Jalil Bounhar 5t. Carnegie Museum of Natural History, Pittsburgh, PA: 14–15b. Corbis: Annie Griffiths Belt
3; Bettmann 16b, 19br, 20b, 21t; Didier Dutheil 15tl; Derek Hall/Frank Lane Picture Agency 8bl; Layne Kennedy 25t; Richard T. Nowitz 30;
Stapleton Collection 7br. DK Images: 11bl; Jon Hughes 11t. Kobal Collection: Amblin/Universal 28–29b. Museum of the Rockies: 22, 23t, 26b, 27t.
The Natural History Museum, London: 11br. Louie Psihoyos ©psihoyos.com: 28t. University of Queensland: Scott Hucknull 20tr. Science Photo
Library: 6tl, 13br; Sheila Terry 13t. Smithsonian Institution: Credit line: National Museum of Natural History ©2003 Smithsonian Institution 1.
Jacket: Corbis: Annie Griffiths Belt front t. Louie Psihoyos ©psihoyos.com: front b.

All other images: DK Dorling Kindersley © 2004. For further information see www.dkimages.com
Dorling Kindersley Ltd., 80 Strand, London WC2R ORL

Contents

Scientists discover the remains of
a ten-million-year-old rhinoceros
in Nebraska, USA.

Discovering Fossils

Imagine leaving the classroom and stepping back in time to the age when dinosaurs walked on Earth. You look around. Many unfamiliar plants and insects surround you. A strange noise startles you, you turn around. Suddenly, you are face to face with a real live dinosaur.

Of course, this could never happen. Dinosaurs are **extinct**. They all died millions of years ago. So how do we know so much about dinosaurs if no one has ever seen one?

A *Giganotosaurus* dinosaur was about three times as large as a modern crocodile.

One way we have found out about dinosaurs is through fossils. Fossils are the remains of once-living things. Sometimes, bones, teeth, skin and footprints are preserved in the layers of rocks that make up the Earth. Scientists who study fossils are called **palaeontologists** (pay-lee-on-TOH-luh-jihsts). This book is about three palaeontologists who helped to bring the past to life.

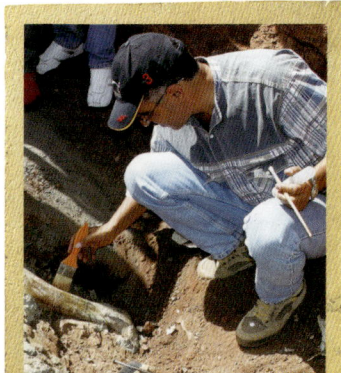

Palaeontologists at Work

Palaeontologists on a "dig" in Morocco use hammers, chisels and brushes to search for clues about the past. It is slow work. Sometimes it takes years to collect enough bones to put together a dinosaur skeleton.

Mary Anning

1799–1847

Birthplace:
Lyme Regis, Dorset

Discovered:
The first plesiosaur fossil

Mary Anning was born in Lyme Regis, Dorset, in 1799. During the 1800s, people found strange things in the ground, but often didn't know what they were. Some looked like stone snakes. Others looked like teeth or bones made of stone. They were really fossils.

Some people used these fossils as medicine or carried them for luck. Others collected them. Not many people tried to learn what they were or where they came from.

Mary first discovered her love of fossil collecting with her father, Richard Anning. When he wasn't working as a carpenter or cabinetmaker, he collected fossils to earn extra money. Mary enjoyed walking along the beaches and climbing the cliffs with her father, searching for fossils to sell.

Mary's father taught her to clean the fossils carefully. He showed her how to add to their value by polishing them and displaying them well. Mary learned how to sell fossils with the help of her father.

This 1825 painting shows the view across Lyme Bay towards Lyme Regis.

Animal to Fossil

1. When an animal dies, layers of sand or mud quickly bury it.

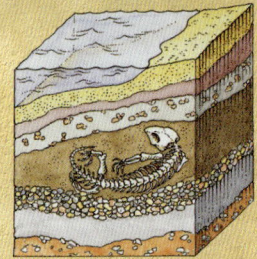

2. Over thousands to millions of years, the layers of mud turn to rock. The animal's skeleton becomes stone-like, as minerals fill spaces or replace the calcium in the bone.

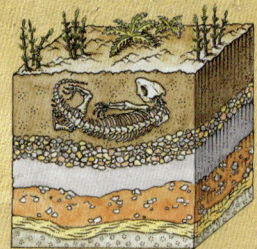

3. The Earth's crust shifts. Buried bones slowly move closer to the surface.

Selling Fossils

When Mary was eleven years old her father died. He left the family with no money. So Mary returned to the shore to look for fossils.

One day Mary found a "snake-stone". It was the fossil of a sea animal that we now call an ammonite. As Mary was taking it home, a woman asked if she could buy it. Mary agreed and earned enough money to buy the family food for a week. After that, Mary and her brother both kept searching for fossils.

Ammonites have coiled shells.

Ammonites once lived in oceans.

One day, Mary's brother found a strange head with huge eyes and lots of teeth. Almost a year later, Mary found the rest of the skeleton. This creature was about 5 metres long. It looked like a fish with ribs similar to a lizard. Years after Mary's discovery, a scientist called the skeleton *Ichthyosaurus* (IHK-thee-uh-SOHR-uhs). A local fossil collector bought this strange fossil from the Annings. He paid Mary and her family enough money to keep them for half a year. Still, Mary and her brother struggled to make a living finding and selling fossils. Sometimes it took days or weeks to dig out and clean one fossil.

Ichthyosaurus means "fish lizard".

This is the skull of an ichthyosaur.

Becoming a Fossil Expert

Mary wanted to know more about the fossils she found. She read everything she could about rocks and learned which rocks most often held fossils.

This knowledge helped Mary recognize the best places to find fossils. She learned that the layers of clay and limestone in the cliffs near her home had once been part of a tropical sea, millions of years before. When the sea water **eroded** the rock on the cliffs, it exposed the fossils of ancient sea creatures.

It was along the cliffs of Lyme Regis that Mary Anning discovered her fossils.

Mary examined how living creatures moved, too. This helped her see how fossilized skeletons were similar to skeletons of living animals.

Over the years, Mary found more ichthyosaur skeletons. She was the first to discover a complete skeleton of a plesiosaur (PLEE-see-oh-sohr). This was another type of ocean reptile. She also found the remains of a flying reptile called *Pterodactylus* (tehr-uh-DAK-tih-luhs).

Pterodactylus means "wing finger".

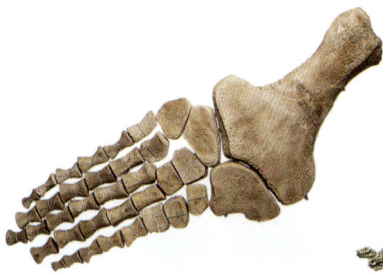

These are the fossilized bones of a plesiosaur's flipper.

Plesiosaurus

Mary Becomes Famous

Mary became an expert at putting fossilized skeletons together. People came to know her because of her talent for finding fossils. Scientists were interested in Mary's work, too. Her fossil discoveries were valuable to them.

Mary helped many people find fossils. Some were scientists who were trying to understand the history of Earth. Mary learned a lot from these scientists, too.

Mary ran a shop in Lyme Regis where she sold the fossils she had collected.

This picture shows how ancient sea life may have looked.

Scientists learned a lot from Mary. Her fossils persuaded them to think about the Earth in new ways. Her discoveries helped people imagine the plants and animals in the seas thousands of years ago. Today many of Mary's fossils are displayed in museums around the world.

Gideon Mantell was another fossil hunter in the 1800s. He visited Mary at her shop in Lyme Regis.

Barnum Brown

1873–1963

Birthplace:
Kansas,
United States

Discovered:
The first fossil of the
dinosaur *Tyrannosaurus rex*

Barnum Brown loved fossils and began collecting them when he was young. He was born in 1873 and grew up to be one of the greatest fossil collectors. Barnum discovered his first fossils in the fields of Kansas in the USA. He followed a farmer's plough and collected fossilized seashells **unearthed** by the plough's blades.

In 1892 Barnum went to the University of Kansas. He was always fascinated by palaeontology. So although he studied the arts and engineering, Barnum loved collecting fossils more than going to his classes.

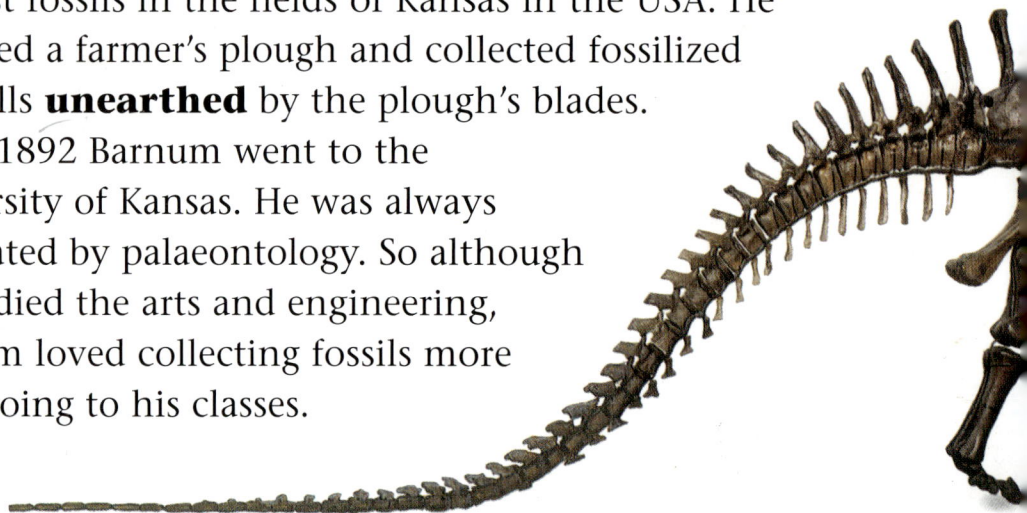

In 1897 Barnum went to work at the American Museum of Natural History in New York City. The director of the museum sent Barnum to look for dinosaur fossils.

Barnum travelled to Wyoming, USA. There he visited a place with so many dinosaur bones that a sheep rancher had built a cabin out of them. While he was there, Barnum discovered an *Apatosaurus* (uh-pat-uh-SOHR-uhs) skeleton. This huge, plant-eating dinosaur once weighed more than 20 tonnes and measured 21 metres long.

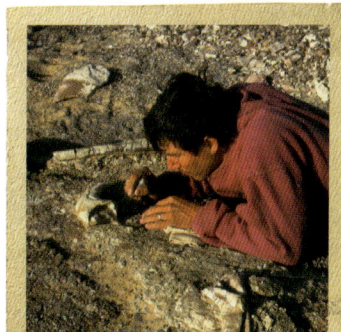

Dinosaur Inspiration
In 1997 a **palaeontologist** called Paul Sereno examined the claw of a newly-discovered dinosaur in the Sahara Desert. Paul first became interested in dinosaurs in the late 1970s when he visited the American Museum of Natural History.

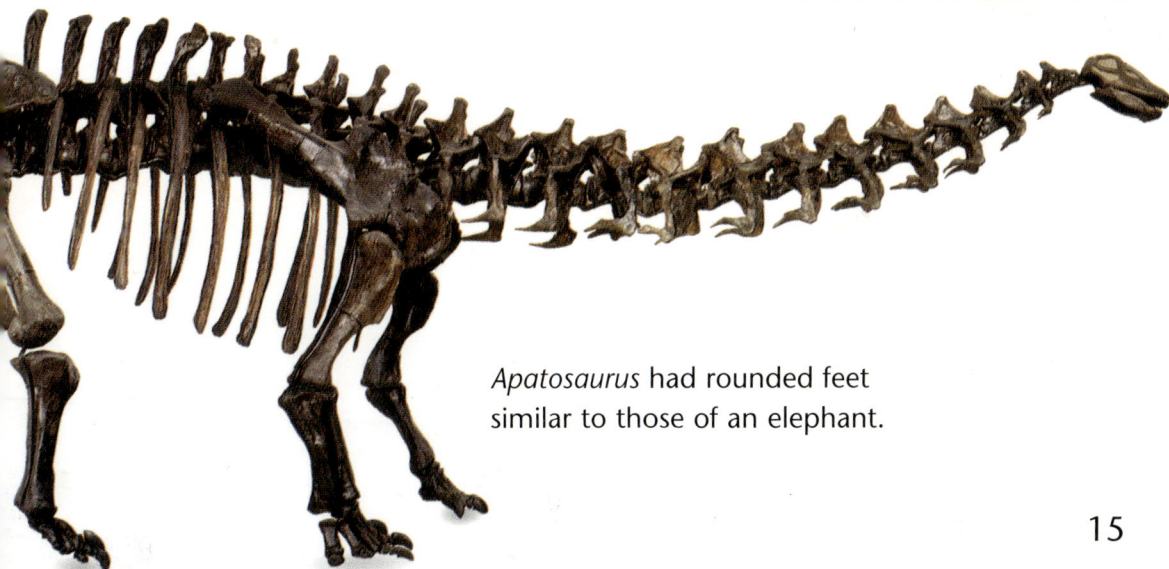

Apatosaurus had rounded feet similar to those of an elephant.

Travelling Fossil Seeker

After three years of fossil hunting, Barnum returned to New York. His discoveries were taken to the American Museum of Natural History and put on display. As soon as Barnum returned, the Museum Director asked him to search for more fossils in South America. He agreed, and had three hours to get ready.

Barnum wrote in his diary, "Imagine getting an outfit [a group of people] together in three hours to go on a 7,000-mile journey, and be gone for a year or more."

This picture shows Barnum Brown (left) discussing a *Triceratops* skeleton with another scientist.

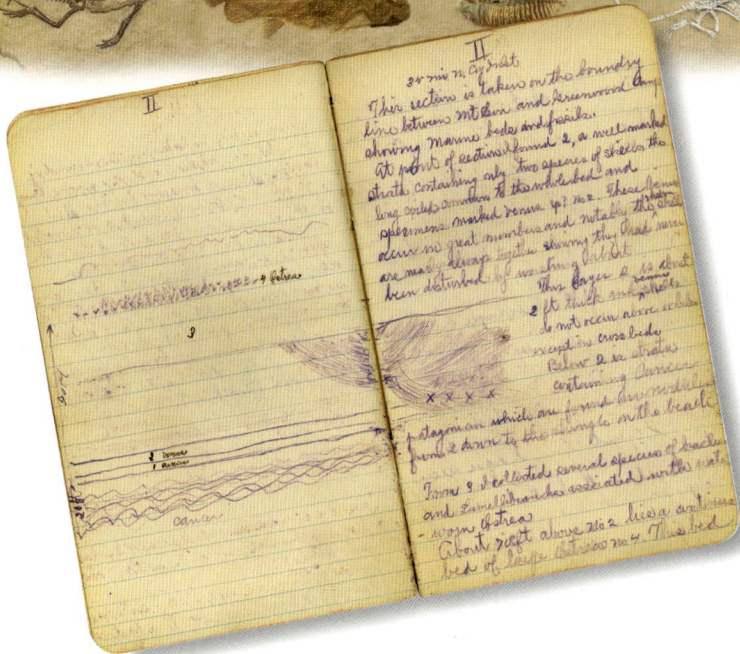

Barnum kept detailed records on his fossil-hunting trips.

Barnum spent more than a year in South America but didn't discover any major fossils. When Barnum returned to the United States, his friend showed him a fossil he had found in eastern Montana, USA. Barnum recognized it as part of the horn of a *Triceratops* (try-SEHR-uh-tops). Barnum packed his bags again and set off for Montana.

While in Montana, Barnum found many fossils, including a *Triceratops* skull and duckbill dinosaur skeletons. He also found the buried skeleton of a huge animal. Using pickaxes, shovels and chisels, Barnum and his crew dug out the fossils. It took them several months to collect all the remains.

Triceratops, means "three-horned face".

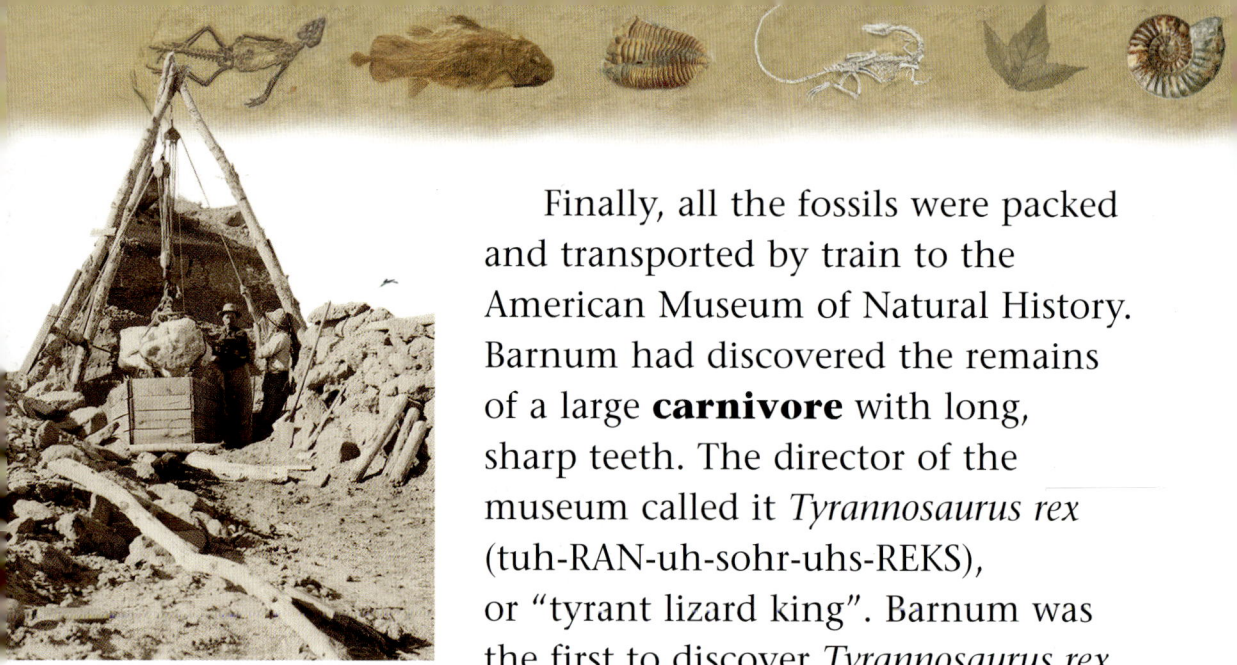

Finally, all the fossils were packed and transported by train to the American Museum of Natural History. Barnum had discovered the remains of a large **carnivore** with long, sharp teeth. The director of the museum called it *Tyrannosaurus rex* (tuh-RAN-uh-sohr-uhs-REKS), or "tyrant lizard king". Barnum was the first to discover *Tyrannosaurus rex*.

Barnum went out and searched for more bones. In 1908 he found another *Tyrannosaurus rex* skeleton. This time it had a complete skull.

Once the carnivore fossils had been excavated, they were placed in wooden crates to be transported to the museum.

Barnum (right) worked with other scientists to carefully put the fossils back together.

This group of fossil seekers wore veils for protection against insects on the Red Deer River.

In 1910 Barnum heard about a new area to explore in Canada. Hillsides had been eroded along the Red Deer River in Alberta. This had exposed many fossils. Barnum and his crew set off again. When Barnum arrived, he found many tonnes of bones. Some belonged to undiscovered dinosaurs. Again, he shipped all his finds back to the museum.

In the 1920s Barnum travelled around the world. He continued discovering fossils. Barnum's wife, Lilian, went with him on many of his explorations. She wrote three books about their work and adventures.

Lilian Brown often went fossil hunting with her husband, Barnum.

Barnum's Fossil Collection

During the 1930s Barnum returned to Montana and Wyoming. There he and his crew found many dinosaur fossils. Most of these were the remains of sauropods (SOHR-uh-podz), with long necks and huge bodies. It seemed as if a whole herd of these dinosaurs had died at once.

Barnum wondered how these sauropods had lived and died. Scientists now believe that they died because their water supply dried up.

A Dinosaur Called Elliot
A sauropod was found in Queensland, Australia, in 2001. It was nicknamed Elliot.
Palaeontologist Dr Steve Salisbury (shown above) of Queensland Museum was part of the team that discovered Elliot.

Barnum found these fossils in Wyoming, in 1934. He numbered the bones so the skeleton could be reassembled at the museum.

Barnum spent 35 years working for the American Museum of Natural History.

This is the specimen found by Brown in 1908. It was the first *Tyrannosaurus* skeleton ever built.

Barnum Brown continued working for the American Museum of Natural History until 1942. Even after that, he guided visitors through the fossils. He showed off his collection until his death at eighty-nine years old.

When Barnum started working at the museum, there wasn't a single dinosaur there. Now the American Museum of Natural History has the largest dinosaur collection in the world.

Jack Horner

1943–

Birthplace:
Shelby, Montana,
United States

Discovered:
Fossilized dinosaur nests and
baby duckbill dinosaurs

Jack Horner always loved to discover things. When
he was a boy in Shelby, Montana, USA, he spent time
exploring the outdoors and searching for treasures.
He often found them, too.

School was difficult for Jack, but he loved learning
and always did well in science. After leaving school,
he went to the University of Montana. He took every
geology and palaeontology course he could. Then Jack
started work at the Princeton Museum of Natural History
in New Jersey, USA.

At the museum, Jack was surrounded by many fossils. He cleaned and organized them. Then every summer Jack returned to Montana to find fossils himself.

Jack holds the skull of a *Hypacrosaurus* (hy-PAK-roh-SOHR-uhs) dinosaur.

Jack wanted to know everything about dinosaurs. He wanted to know what they looked like and how they lived. Jack was especially interested in duckbill dinosaurs. He wanted to find bones from baby duckbills, but he didn't know where to look.

Duckbill dinosaurs had broad beaks for stripping leaves from plants.

Jack Horner named the dinosaur that made this nest *Maiasaura* (my-uh-SOHR-uh), which means "good mother lizard".

Discovering "Egg Mountain"

In 1978 Jack visited a rock shop in Bynum, Montana. Inside, the owner had a coffee jar full of fossils. He asked Jack to identify them.

"What I had in my hand," Jack said later, "was a bone from a baby dinosaur, a duckbill – exactly what I wanted, in a place I never expected to find it." The rock shop owner told Jack where she had found the fossils, so he finally knew where to dig.

Jack and a friend started searching the area. There they found whole nests with fossilized babies and eggs in them. They called the area Egg Mountain.

This amazing discovery gave Jack a new understanding of how dinosaurs might have lived. Duckbills didn't act like lizards, as everyone believed. Lizards laid eggs and left them to hatch, but duckbills seemed to care about their hatchlings. The duckbill's behaviour was more bird-like than lizard-like. Jack's fossil discoveries were put on display at the museum in Princeton.

Fossil Collections
All the fossils in a museum collection are organized by **palaeontologists**. First the fossils are cleaned. Then the palaeontologists record important information about each fossil.

Maiasaura seems to have cared for its hatchlings.

Questions and Answers

In 1982 Jack left his job in New Jersey and went to work at the Museum of the Rockies in Montana, USA. He studied and taught at the museum in the winter months but continued to dig for fossils every summer. His findings were put on display at the museum in Montana.

Jack continued to ask questions. How did dinosaurs live? What did they eat? Were they warm-blooded? Did they live in herds? Did they **migrate**? Did they all take care of their young?

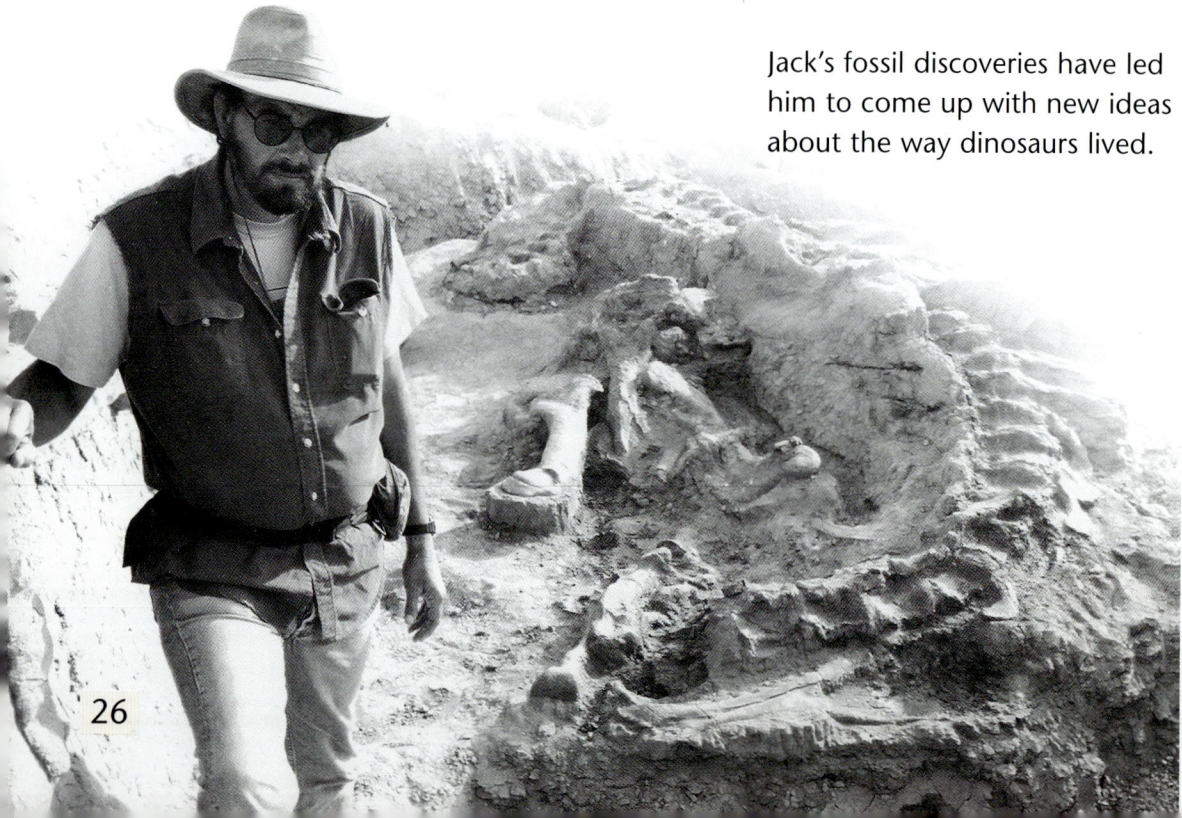

Fighting Dinosaurs
Zofia Kielan-Jaworowska from Poland is a **palaeontologist**. She discovered dinosaur fossils in Mongolia in Asia in 1971. They looked as if they had died while fighting.

Jack's fossil discoveries have led him to come up with new ideas about the way dinosaurs lived.

In 2003 Jack found his eighth *Tyrannosaurus rex*.

To answer questions like these, Jack tried to find as many **species** of dinosaur skeletons as possible. Then he compared the bones of each skeleton to learn how the dinosaurs grew. He also examined the plant and animal fossils in different layers of rocks. This helped him learn about the dinosaurs' **habitats**.

Jack studied the exact position of the fossils when they were discovered. This helped him learn how dinosaurs behaved. He also tried to understand how and why dinosaurs changed over the millions of years they roamed the Earth.

Palaeontologists make maps of fossil finds.

New Ideas About *Tyrannosaurus rex*

In 1990 Jack and his crew dug up another *Tyrannosaurus rex*. For the next few years, they cleaned the bones. Then in 2000, Jack and his crew found five more *Tyrannosaurus rex* skeletons. One was more than 12 metres long. Jack studied the *Tyrannosaurus rex* bones to learn more about this dinosaur's behaviour and habits.

Jack Horner with a *Tyrannosaurus rex* skeleton.

One question Jack is exploring is how *Tyrannosaurus rex* obtained food. Most **palaeontologists** think *Tyrannosaurus rex* was a **predator** who hunted down and killed animals to eat. Jack has a different idea, though. He thinks that *Tyrannosaurus rex* was a **scavenger**. He believes it ate the flesh of dead animals.

Jack keeps searching for the answer. He continues to dig up fossils. He continues to ask questions and search for answers about how dinosaurs lived.

Jack Horner worked on the *Jurassic Park* films.

Discoveries Continue

Palaeontologists share their discoveries, check each other's work and sometimes come to different conclusions. Some of them want to know what dinosaurs looked like. Others are more interested in finding out how dinosaurs behaved. Many want to learn how living things have changed over time. Together these fossil seekers bring the past to life.

These fossil hunters are digging for dinosaur remains at Egg Mountain in Montana.

Glossary

carnivore — a meat-eating animal

extinct — no longer living

habitats — places where plants or animals naturally live

migrate — to move with the seasons

palaeontologists — scientists who study fossils

predator — an animal that captures and eats other animals

scavenger — an animal that eats dead and decaying flesh

species — a group of similar plants or animals

unearthed — dug up from the earth

Index